The Price of Isolation

Harry Harlow and the Science of Love

Freudian Trip

Copyright Page

Disclaimer

The views and opinions expressed in this book are those of the author(s) and do not necessarily reflect the official policy or position of any other agency, organization, employer, or company. The contents of this book are for informational and educational purposes only and are not intended to serve as professional advice, diagnosis, or treatment.

The information provided in this book is believed to be accurate and reliable as of the date of publication. However, it may include some errors or inaccuracies, and no warranty or guarantee is provided regarding the accuracy, timeliness, or applicability of the content.

Readers are encouraged to consult with professional philosophers, educators, or other qualified professionals where appropriate for personalized advice. The author(s) and publisher shall not be liable for any loss, damage, or harm caused or alleged to be caused, directly or indirectly, by the information or ideas contained, suggested, or referenced in this book.

By reading this book, the reader acknowledges and agrees that they are solely responsible for how they interpret and apply the information contained herein.

This book may also include references to other works, studies, and sources. These references are provided for further reading and exploration and do not imply endorsement or validation of the specific theories, viewpoints, or interpretations presented in those works.

Introduction: A Different Kind of Science

Before the middle of the 20th century, most scientists who studied children acted like serious detectives focused only on the facts. Could a baby see? Could they follow instructions? Did they get enough to eat? Love, cuddling, and playtime seemed like fluffy stuff, not important for scientific investigation. They believed if you fed a child, clothed them, and taught them right from wrcng, everything else would fall into place.

But one scientist, Harry Harlow, suspected there was a missing piece of the puzzle. He looked at babies, both human and animal, and saw something besides hunger and basic needs. He saw a spark of connection. Harlow didn't just have a theory; he was determined to prove that love was as real and as vital as food itself. Of course, you can't exactly ask a baby how they feel about their mom. So, Harlow turned to an unlikely source for answers: monkeys.

Harlow wasn't some cuddly animal lover– he was a brilliant, sometimes stubborn researcher. His journey wasn't about proving that love is warm and fuzzy. It was about cold, hard science. He wanted to measure it, define it, and show that what happens in those early moments between a parent and child has a lifelong effect.

His experiments would turn out to be shocking, even a bit cruel at times. Yet, his results changed the way we think about how babies grow, not just physically, but emotionally too.

Chapter 1: A Mother's Choice

Picture this: a tiny baby monkey, eyes wide and curious, alone in a cage. There are two figures that could be its mother. One is made of cold, hard wire. But, this wire mother has something important – a bottle of milk. The other "mother" is different. She has no food, but she's built from soft, comforting cloth. This is the choice Harry Harlow gave to his baby monkeys.

Now, you might think this is an easy decision. Food equals survival, right? But Harlow was about to make a startling discovery. These baby monkeys clung tightly to the cloth mother, even when they were desperately hungry. They'd only venture to the wire mother long enough to grab the milk, then scurry right back for the comfort of the soft cloth.

Why was this happening? Before Harlow, most scientists would have scoffed at the idea that a monkey could feel "love." But as Harlow watched their behavior, he started to believe otherwise. The baby monkeys ran to the cloth mother when they were scared. They nestled against her for warmth and security. They seemed to find something in the softness that no amount of milk could replace.

Harlow proved it wasn't about the practical stuff, like food. It was about a feeling– a deep need for connection and comfort. The baby monkeys taught us that a mother's love isn't just a nice extra, it is an essential building block for healthy growth. Food keeps the body alive, but touch, it seemed, could nourish a monkey's very soul.

Chapter 2: Cages of Silence

Harry Harlow's first experiments revealed the power of a mother's touch. But his journey into the mysteries of a baby's heart was far from over. His next question was dark and troubling: What happens if there's no comfort at all?

Harlow designed special cages that would cut a baby monkey off from the world. No soft cloth, no wire mothers, not even a glimpse of another monkey. These babies lived in total isolation. Day after day, they existed in a silent world, their only company their own reflection.

The results were devastating. As the monkeys grew, it became clear that something inside them was broken. Unlike normally raised monkeys who were playful and curious, the isolated monkeys were terrified. Some huddled in a corner, rocking back and forth. Others showed fits of rage, biting at their own hands or lashing out at anything that came near.

When placed with other monkeys, they didn't know what to do. There was no joyful playing, no friendly grooming. They either cowered in fear or attacked without reason. Later on, as adults, they struggled with the most basic aspects of being a monkey. None of the isolated females could figure out how to mate, and even if they had babies, they were often neglectful or even abusive mothers.

Harlow had uncovered a terrible truth: the need for love isn't just about feeling good. Early social experiences are woven into the very fabric of who we become. They teach us how to interact, how to cope with big emotions, and even how to be parents ourselves. Isolation robs a creature of these fundamental skills. It's more than sadness; it's like trying to learn to speak without ever hearing a word.

Chapter 3: Can a Broken Heart Mend?

Harry Harlow wasn't a monster. His experiments hurt those baby monkeys deeply, and he knew it. But he also had a flicker of hope. Could the damage he'd observed be reversed? Could love, introduced later, finally heal the wounds inflicted by those lonely cages?

He tried several things. One of his most interesting ideas was using "therapist monkeys." These were exceptionally playful and good-natured monkeys, placed with the isolated ones to see if they could teach them social skills through patience and gentle interaction. He also tried simply putting young, isolated monkeys together, hoping shared experience might help them learn what they'd missed.

There was some success. Over time, a few isolated monkeys showed improvement. The most fearful began to cautiously explore. Some even seemed to form tentative friendships with their peers. But a truly normal life always seemed out of reach. They were awkward, easily startled. And the mothers who'd been raised in isolation never fully grasped how to nurture their own babies.

Harlow's rehabilitation attempts revealed a heartbreaking reality. The window for developing certain skills and emotional security is tragically small. Some damage, especially inflicted very early in life, can leave scars that never completely fade. Yet, his work also showed the incredible power of connection. Even a little bit of kindness and social exposure seemed better than none at all.

Chapter 4: The Cost of Discovery

Harry Harlow changed the way we see children forever. Before his wire mothers and lonely cages, love seemed too fluffy, too subjective for serious scientific study. Harlow showed that emotional bonds have real, measurable consequences. His work helped change the way orphanages and hospitals were run. No longer was it acceptable to just feed and clothe babies; staff were encouraged to hold, play, and provide loving touch.

Yet, his legacy will always be stained with controversy. Looking at pictures of his experiments today, it's hard not to feel a pang of sympathy for those frightened baby monkeys. Many would argue that the knowledge Harlow gained was never worth the suffering he caused. Was it right to inflict such pain in the name of science?

This is the ethical price tag to Harlow's work – there's no easy answer. His research sparked greater awareness about the emotional health of animals, and stricter rules now exist on what kinds of experiments can be done. But the debate continues: does the potential for human benefit ever justify harming another creature?

Harlow's findings influence how we think about our own lives too. When a parent neglects a child, or someone grows up without love, the consequences are now understood as more than emotional. This early deprivation can influence both physical and mental development throughout life.

Harry Harlow was a complicated figure. He could be harsh and sometimes seemed unmoved by the distress in his lab. Yet, his work revealed a hidden truth: we are creatures shaped by love. It's a need as fundamental as the hunger for food, and its absence leaves scars that science may never fully understand how to heal.

Chapter 5: The Bonds That Shape Us

Harry Harlow's experiments were a powerful wake-up call, but they were just the beginning. Inspired by his work, a British psychiatrist named John Bowlby dug deeper into the patterns of how babies and parents bond. He gave a name to this phenomenon: Attachment Theory.

Bowlby believed that we're all born with a biological drive to connect with a caregiver. When babies feel safe, responded to, and loved, they develop a sense of "secure attachment." This gives them the confidence to explore the world, knowing there's always a safe place to return to. But when babies experience neglect or inconsistency, they can develop anxious or avoidant attachment styles, making it harder to trust and form healthy relationships later on.

Modern science backs this idea up in a big way. Studies using brain scans now show that early experiences literally shape how the brain develops. Securely attached children have stronger connections in areas related to emotional regulation and social skills.

This has real-world implications. Harlow's work helped convince the world that babies in orphanages needed more than clean diapers. Today, we debate things like the importance of paid parental leave so new parents can form those vital early bonds. It fuels research into how to make childcare settings not just safe, but actively nurturing for very young brains.

Of course, it's not all doom and gloom if you had a rough childhood. Our brains are amazingly adaptable. Positive relationships throughout life can help heal some of those early hurts. But Harlow's legacy reminds us that the best time to help a child is in the very beginning, when their hearts and minds are wide open, soaking in everything that love has to teach.

Conclusion: The Scientist Who Taught Us About Love

Harry Harlow was a man of contradictions. He could be dismissive of the baby monkeys in his care, seeing them as tools for his science, not individuals. Yet, the very cruelty of his experiments revealed a profound truth: love is a force as powerful as any physical need.

His legacy is stained by the suffering he caused. It's impossible to look at the pictures of his isolated monkeys without discomfort. His work makes us ask uncomfortable questions about where we draw the line between the pursuit of knowledge and the compassion we owe all living creatures.

Yet, Harlow's findings cannot be ignored. They forever changed the landscape of how we raise and view children. Hospitals redesigned their care for babies, orphanages shifted their focus, and parents themselves became more aware of the immense power of their touch and attention.

His work also reminds us that science doesn't exist in a vacuum. The choices scientists make, driven by either curiosity or ambition, can ripple outwards in unexpected ways. Harlow forced us to look at the dark spaces within our own hearts – was the knowledge gained worth the pain inflicted along the way?

Perhaps ultimately, Harlow's most important lesson wasn't just about how monkeys or even humans need love. It was a reminder that science, for all its brilliance, needs a moral compass. Discoveries are empty if they are built on a foundation of suffering without purpose.

Appendix: Beyond the Monkey Cages: Love Across the Animal Kingdom

Harry Harlow's wire mothers and isolated monkeys caused a shockwave. Yet, the need for love and connection doesn't just belong to us primates. Across the animal kingdom, creatures form bonds, nurture their young, and suffer loss in ways that eerily mirror our own experiences.

- **Our Primate Cousins:** Harlow's focus was on rhesus macaques, with whom we share a common ancestor. But the impact of social isolation can be even more pronounced in chimpanzees or bonobos. These apes live in complex communities with deep friendships and family ties. Taking away those connections can leave wounds more devastating than those Harlow inflicted.
- **Songs of Attachment:** Birds might sing rather than hug, but their need for companionship is equally powerful. Many species form lifelong bonds, their calls a complex language of care and devotion. Nestlings

deprived of parental warmth and interaction struggle to thrive, mirroring Harlow's cloth-mother discoveries.

- **The Canine Connection:** Dogs, through centuries of domestication, have become uniquely tuned to human emotion. Their joyful greetings and comforting presence are more than just cute tricks. Studies show that dogs truly offer stress relief, mirroring Harlow's discovery that touch can soothe a troubled spirit. The importance of puppy socialization shows us that healthy emotional development in dogs relies on early social experiences, just like human children.

Harlow primarily focused on monkeys, revealing the depths of their suffering. But by looking across the animal kingdom, his work gains even greater weight. It forces us to recognize that we are not unique in our need to belong. Love, in its many forms, might be the most fundamental biological drive of them all.

About Freudian Trips

Welcome to Freudian Trips, your dedicated platform for diving deep into the world of psychology. We are more than just a YouTube channel or a book publisher. We are a beacon of enlightenment, making complex psychological concepts accessible and engaging for all.

Our YouTube channel is a rich repository of psychology made simple. We take the profound and often complex ideas from the world of psychology and break them down into digestible, easy-to-understand content. From the foundational theories of Freud to the cognitive insights of Piaget, we cover a broad spectrum of psychological schools and thoughts, making psychology accessible to everyone, regardless of their background or prior knowledge.

As a book publisher, we take the same approach, transforming intricate psychological theories into comprehensible narratives. Our books are not just collections of words, but vessels of wisdom that make psychology approachable and relatable. We believe that psychology should not be confined to academic circles, but should be available to all who seek to understand the human mind and behavior.

At Freudian Trips, we believe in the power of curiosity and the pursuit of knowledge. We are here to stoke the fires of your curiosity, to guide you on your intellectual journey, and to help you navigate the fascinating world of psychology.

If you are someone who is not afraid to question, to explore, and to learn, then you are in the right place. Join us on this journey of exploration, as we make psychology easy to understand, one concept at a time.

Be sure to visit our Youtube channel at:
www.freudiantrips.com/youtube

You can also visit us on the web at www.freudiantrips.com

Welcome to The Freudian Trip community. Stay curious. Stay enlightened.